AF488155

The Christmas Lesson:

Unwrapping Love and Family

The Rules of a Big Boss LLC
Knightdale, NC 27545

Dedication

Dear Reader,

May the pages of "The Christmas Lesson" fill your hearts with the warmth of love, the joy of family, and the wonder of the holiday season.

As you embark on this journey, I hope that you discover that the true treasures of Christmas lie not just in presents, but in the laughter, the stories, and the bonds that we share.

Wishing you a season filled with love, laughter, and endless moments that shine brightly, like the stars in a winter sky.

With love and holiday magic,

Dedrick

Once upon a time, in a small city called Greensboro, there lived a mischievous little boy named Lamar. He loved Christmas more than anything in the world. Lamar adored the twinkling lights, the scent of freshly baked cookies, and the joy in the air. But what he loved most was sneaking around to find his hidden Christmas gifts.

Lamar's eyes would dance with curiosity and mischief every year as the familiar melody of "Silent Night" by the Temptations played on the radio. His mom, Renee, had a special talent for hiding gifts in the sneakiest places, and Lamar couldn't resist the challenge of uncovering them.

Even though Lamar knew that snooping around was wrong, the
thrill of discovering his gifts was just too much fun to resist.
He would secretly listen to Renee's hushed conversations
hoping to catch any hints about where his gifts might be hiding.

One snowy December morning, as he was playing with his
Transformers, Lamar overheard Renee talking to his uncle,
Lavon. She said, "I hid Lamar's bike in the place he loves
the most," with a hushed chuckle. His eyes sparkled with
delight because he knew exactly where it was hidden.

Trying to contain his excitement, Lamar waited until Renee was fast asleep before tiptoeing up the stairs and into the attic. He laughed to himself as he searched every corner, but the bike was nowhere to be found.

Lamar wasn't about to give up, though. He needed to think like the world's greatest detective, Batman. Seated on his bed, Lamar thought hard. Then a brilliant idea struck him. Renee said the gift was in the place he loved most. And where was that? His granny, Mae's house, of course!

With a mischievous grin, Lamar called Mae and told her how much he missed her. He asked if he could come over and help decorate her house for Christmas. Mae happily agreed.

With bubbling excitement, Lamar jumped out of the car
as they reached Mae's house. He dashed to the storage
room, where he spotted mysterious boxes tucked away in
the corner. His heart raced as he reached for them.
Inside one of them was the coolest bike he had ever
seen. It was red and black all over. Lamar couldn't help
but grin from ear to ear.

But just as he was lost in awe of his new bike, Lamar heard Mae's voice calling, "Lamar, where are you?" In his rush to leave the storage room, he accidentally knocked over not only the bike but a bunch of other gifts too.

Mae heard the commotion and asked, "Lamar, were you sneaking around in the storage room?" With a deep sigh, Lamar confessed, "Yes, Granny." Mae smiled gently and asked, "And what did you find?" Lamar admitted, "I found my bike and lots of Christmas gifts, Granny."

Mae let out a sigh, a mix of understanding and gentle disappointment. She said, "I should tell your mom about this, but I'll keep it our little secret for now." She invited him into the house, and they had a heart-to-heart conversation as they decorated the Christmas Tree together.

Mae shared her own past, how she didn't have much money when Renee, Lavon, and the rest of his aunts and uncles were younger. With a sparkle in her eye, she gently shared that back then, gifts were few, but there was an abundance of something even more precious, love. In her warm and wise way, Mae explained that Christmas was a celebration of the birth of Jesus, a time to wrap our hearts in love, and a time to gather with family. From that very moment, Lamar decided to embrace patience and eagerly await the sunrise of Christmas morning.

Each day, Lamar's excitement grew stronger as he looked
forward to opening presents and spending time with his
loved ones. Lamar's heart raced as he dashed downstairs on
Christmas morning. The tree was a shimmering wonderland,
surrounded by gifts everywhere.

Lamar tore into his boxes of new toys and clothes but most of
all he was excited about his new bike. He couldn't wait to go
outside and show it to his friends. As Lamar turned around, he
saw Mae and Renee wiping away tears of happiness while his
aunts and uncles exchanged gifts and shared stories. At last,
he fully understood. Christmas wasn't just about receiving
gifts; it was about sharing joy with family.

And so, in the little city of Greensboro, the mischievous little boy named Lamar learned the true spirit of Christmas. He never again tried to sneak around for gifts, cherishing instead the magic of the holiday and the love that surrounded him.

Or did he?

THE END

Conclusion

Christmas isn't just about the presents we receive, it's about the love that we share with our family and friends. Lamar's mischievous adventure taught him that the joy of Christmas comes from being patient, spending time with loved ones, and cherishing the special moments together.

Much like Lamar, we might feel excited to uncover surprises, but the true magic of the holiday season lies in the bonds we build and the memories we create. As you celebrate this festive occasion, remember that the warmth of love, the twinkle of togetherness, and the joy of giving are the greatest gifts of all.

Wishing you all the love and magic this holiday season has to offer.

Dedrick L. Moone

Acknowledgments

I would like to thank God for His gifts that renew daily. I love you from the soles of my feet to the tip of my head.

I would like to honor my granny, Beulah M. Moone. You are my forever best friend. I will love you always.

I would like to acknowledge my mom, Wanda R. Moone. You did more than any parent could do, and you did it on your own. I love and appreciate you.

I would like to thank my pop, Terrance (Terry) R. Westry. You accepted and loved me as your eldest son whereas my actual father did not. I love you always.

I would like to acknowledge my uncle, Anthony (Tony) R. Moone. You were my very first father figure and superhero. I love you.

I would like to honor my uncle, Wesley (Wes) J. Moone. You have always been there with sage advice, good jokes, and a timely gift. I love you.

I would like to thank and acknowledge my wife, Dr. Vanessa R. Moone. You are truly my helpmeet and 31st Psalm Lady. I love you with all my heart.

I would like to thank my daughter, Haelee P. Moone. You helped me find my strength and you love me without conditions. I love you with all my heart, Little Moone.

I unfortunately do not have enough space to acknowledge everyone. But do know that you are loved, appreciated, and valued beyond words.

BIO PAGE

Dear reader,

Dedrick L. Moone is a dedicated individual who wears many hats and possesses a genuine passion for making a positive impact. As a loving husband and proud girl-dad, he finds joy and fulfillment in his family life. Dedrick's roles as an author, philanthropist, humanitarian, book reviewer, international motivational speaker, and Toastmaster allow him to inspire and uplift others.

Driven by his desire to see individuals thrive, Dedrick's life's mission centers around creating a positive and enjoyable impact wherever he goes. He embraces a diverse range of hobbies, including writing, working out, designing products, marketing, vision boarding, and reading. Additionally, he cherishes quality time spent with his wife, daughter, and their beloved dog.

Dedrick's remarkable journey has been recognized and celebrated through numerous features on reputable news channels such as WCNC News, WGHP News, Spectrum 1 News, ABC 11 News, and WRAL News. His wisdom and insights have also reached a global audience through podcast appearances.

Dedrick's commitment to continuous learning and community involvement is reflected in his memberships and affiliations with esteemed organizations such as Literacy Nation, American Library Association (ALA), Independent Book Publishers Association (IBPA), Alliance of Independent Authors (ALLi), Toastmasters, Sistahs Who Care, and Primplife. Furthermore, his educational background includes graduation from North Carolina A&T State University, a testament to his dedication to personal growth and development.

With his multifaceted talents, infectious enthusiasm, and strong values, Dedrick L. Moone remains a source of inspiration for many. He continues to impact lives through his various endeavors, leaving a lasting legacy of positivity, empowerment, and a love for learning.

Contact the Author

You can connect or contact Dedrick via social media or the web. Details are provided below. He hopes to hear from you.

 https://www.thebookofselflove.com

 @The Rules of a Big Boss

 @DMoone78

 @DMoone78

 @DMoone78

Also by Dedrick L. Moone

Joy Comes: A Story of Fatherhood

Dear Daughter: A Love Story

Don't Let it Ruin the Life of the Party

The Unexpected Journey: Fire and Gold